100 MOMENTS

100 Moments

SERAPHINA TAYLOR

Cover by Harry Hudson Taylor

CONTENTS

Pins And Needles
79

78 Please Go Abroad Before My Heart Breaks
80

Pondering Ponderosa
81

Pop By At Work
83

Post-Vaccine Flu
84

Rapeseed Fields And Infant Wheat
85

Red Veins
86

Research
87

Running Down Stairs
89

Salmon Tartare at Cerna Moderna
90

Sauv' Blanc Les Fumées Blanches Lurton
91

Skin On Spuds
92

Stabbing Nails
93

Sunset Salad
94

The Broccoli In Our Living Room
95

The Children Won't Commute
96

The First Morning Together Again
98

The Lost Art Of Hembraiding
99

The Love Of A Friend
100

The Old Ache Of Insecurity
102

The Plight Of 1 Ply
103

The Rust On Grandpa's Tin Tools
104

A SIMPLE BRUNCH

Strawberries
Wild innocence
Omnipotently, unpolitically loved

We burst their juicy kisses
With our sun-soaked mouths
Letting sweetness, a moment
Soften our morning

Mellowing deadlines
Cancelling calls
Extra time melting
With our margarine
Into lovecrafted bread

Splitting the luxury
Of half an avocado in three
To chew between sips
From cat-shaped coffee cups
All on a Wednesday morning

A TIME FOR SMELLING

It arises, warm,
The smell of honey
Balancing aloft
The growing summer
Of a May day

It snakes up
Green and yellow
Like vine-fresh leaves
Gently winding
Up the senses

Smooth and languid
Yet crisp and sweet
Bounteous flowers
Lifting scent

Holding to my nose
A morning greeting

AGAINST THE KITCHEN COUNTER

My arms wraps her waist
Lips search her neck
Fingers race her back
Bareskin bursting from her jumpsuit
Holy, hot body

The warm, luscious touch
Pulls my desirous digits
Lures my hands
Down the supple swoop
Of her cotton-covered hips

To the throbbing rub
Of her lace-embraced pussy

BEFORE YOU'RE OUT THE BELLY

You have been so loved
So nurtured, so nourished
A whole being and biology
As a medium for birth

For the last nine months
You've grown her into a mother
And she's held herself
As wholly your home

Softening her edges
Strengthening your cradle
Making sure her body
Is ready to move you above belly

It's only the beginning
Her love will expand
Everywhere you go
And to all that you do

Her body, mind and soul
Have been remade just for you

BIKE LINE

A dark ribbon of mulch
Barely a foot wide
Laid low leaf line
One continuous tyre
Cycling on for miles
Each churn of the spokes
Mashes leaves more
Turning tender veins to mortar
Squeezed between citrus colour
Stripes of fallen life

Perhaps it's nature's graceful version
Of an accidental melted edge
Where some clumsy person
Rushing, hot
Iron in hand
Flicks a burn
Into polyester patchwork
Thinly blanketing the earth
Singeing a ribbon
Of packed plant paste
Threaded along the coated ground

Here is a scar the humans run
Here is a tide mark of cycle-scum
Bike line

BLUE

Alien blue
That's what he thought
A spaceship cable
Bungee corded
Ready to snap baby back
Recoil from his futility
Slurp back to safety
From his impune, unimportant
Imp arms

Somehow his wife, arms and all, had grown
To take up the whole hospital room
Giant baby cradle breasts
Full house belly
Garage vagina
Reversing a baby out the entrance
Seemingly secretly
Having always been an exit
Of woman's hidden miracles
Man could merely prod at
To be confirmed into fatherhood

Dad, a baulk, a blubbering bystander
A bollard pedestrian in the way
Peeks in to see the black headlights
Of baby backed out
Receiving his blessing
An experience he feels first hand

Then heart
Instead of mediated through the walls
Of her housing

All of a sudden, out of the blue
He is overwhelmed, whilst everyone works
As this colourful experience comes to light
He's handed scissors

"Cut the cord"

How will Baby get back if I can't handle this?
He snips through the bungee
Marvelling at its slippery perfection
He's begun a belly button
Now the colour seems like heaven
Sky blue

BLUE-EYED SEABREEZE

Sea breeze knocking my knees
Shivers over my skin.
Wind in my hair
Stirring your stare
Our thoughts purr from within.

The cold bites, jaw clenches
Thoughts are tough to chew
But swallow them down
Bring your body around
To this rolling view.

A gull flies on the wind of its cries
A sky of blissful blue.
But I'm watching no more
Than the blue of the shore
That rolls in the eyes of you.

BOUNTIFUL

At my flat, I grow a single lemon
It hangs low, on a little tree
Desperate for light
In the living room

But here, my girlfriend's growing home,
Her parents harvest its siblings
Jutting, turgid and juicy
Sun-soaked citrus
Crowning the backdrop of homespun hair
Flowing yellow from my girl's head

Their fruit makes no statement, not out of place
Not a necessary injection of life
To an old Berlin flat
It simply goes with the rapeseed scenery
The fields of green
The cultivated grass
That pad-soft carpet
Blanketing each step
Over flower-speckled living space
In her parent's garden
There's a slow comfort to growing here
Everything has its time to ripen
Including my girl
There's warm weather and sundress air

A fish gups and interrupts my thoughts
Playing in the pond

Looking up, her lemon edge disappears
Into the flower field
Merging back into its bounty

BREAD TO REMEMBER

Its stony edge catches my finger
Like a curious hand wandering free
On a whole-sky hike
To touch the fresh surface of slow-grown morning
Dewy on this warm rock

It holds the brown ground crunch
Of bracken based winter walks
Crackling after the hidden sun
Behind the oven door horizon

It touches our noses with a waking kiss
Of the homeliest aroma
Bread's stomach-hugging scent

Then I break into thick, chewy indulgence
The whiskey oak char crust
Then subtly sweet bouncy chomp
The tender woody flavours
Building delicious foundations
Of a breakfast moment
Shared in the impermanence
Of this golden freshness

Grown over an earth's spin
Baked over a sunrise
This bread was loved into being

BROTH

The woolley warmth
Of a tartan hearth
Comforts against the cold

Fulfilling like family
With a salty scratch
In a clan of flavours

Blood-thick taste
Earthen edges melt
In a stocky broth
Every sip heartfelt

CAFE LANDTMANN'S ENGLISH MUFFIN

This English muffin and coil of butter
Sophisticate the simple
Smooth table top
Surface marbled
Supports culinary acts
Performing upon its stage
Its warm oak melts dairy
Semi-sever its pale middle
Unveil frothy ribbons of white
Peel open; an aromatic book
Fill the senses with stories
Of how the chef crafted the scent
From impassioned years
Of love-fingered kneading
Hand-modelling the history
Of this muffin's ancestors
Raising leavened life
Sweet pillow tenderness
Of bliss-flavoured bread

CAULIFLOWER SOUP IN PRAGUE

Here is a soup
Puréed cauliflower, coconut mylk
Toasted seeds, oil
Presented in a simple bowl
With a simple spoon

But the complex florets blend
So carefully in cloud-tasting
Mylk fresh from the sky
Without the tinny edge
Of mass production

Every dissolved grain of salt,
Vegetal fibre,
Every thick oil drop
Metamorphosing to soft umami

Gently it slides
Peppered with toasted flakes
Smokey cos-sine tasty peaks
Of seeded crunch
Down to a soft vibe
Transforming my insides
To a warmly murmured "mmmmmmm...."

CHILDHOOD BEDROOM

Your skin soft and smooth
Relaxed in your familial home
Returning to a place of self acceptance
There's no need to forge a path
Or use this time
For anything but lie-ins

There's no need to correct the clocks
Or capture precisely
The start of spring
Warmth is always somewhere
Stood and stable, merely shifting
From patio to fire place

It ebbs with hours
A gentle joy
As if we are as established
As we ever need to be
Just by taking time here

There's an unspoken ease to living
As if breathing is always slow
In this childhood space
To rush is to blaspheme
Against the welcome
We are to savour this time
Cracked open for slow nibbling
With occasional nods to recognise

Its special delight
Silently saying "how well you make us fit here"

I hold you and your childhood
Tenderly. Slowly trailing
Every murmur-inducing plane
Of your whole-grown self
A little moisture lifts to meet my trickling fingers
And I pace my touch
To match your trembling breaths
Not wanting to rush your excitement
I host your happiness in my arms
Creating a new homecoming
Within the wall-to-wall echoes of your past
But I try not to punctuate the moment
Try to slide from long and gradual waking up
To duvet-thick held breaths
Still giving you the slowness
To smell your teenage sheets

"Feel at home" my hands urge
Whilst the sumptuous comfort
Of the skin on skin I bring
Is unavoidably new
To your old bed

I'm hoping to blend in with your bedding
And be just another at breakfast
Without bringing "forever"s or "I do"s
To silently make your coffee
The way you like it
Without disturbing anyone
To ask where the filters are

I am your first
Present-to-parents girlfriend
And I want the weekend
To keep your skin soft

To find your back relaxed
With each brush of my supporting hand
The love of your parents
To fit with mine
Without me wanting to prove how much I love you
I do, I'm here, holding you
As I will a million times more

But in this moment, wrapped in your past
Tickled by your future
I want to let time slide,
To make no divide,
To be altogether present

COFFEE KAKA

I have a magic power
To sleep post-espresso
Or to tolerate a thousand shots
Retaining corporal calm
Keeping my head ache-free

But whilst all seems still
Composed and poised
My coffee drinking causes
A tummy-bound chaos
That leads me trembling to the toilet
To release caffeinated kakas in the Klo

How dramatically coffee promotes peristalsis
Powering through the knotted ribbons of my gut
To move my bowels around
Producing brown from brown
Pouring everything out my butt

DANCING IN SECURITY

Save these four minutes
For your body
To secretly indulge

Use the magic of movement
To spell out who you are
In hip-sway letters, shoulder-roll words

Eyes closed in an elevator
Or in a cross-carpet shuffle
Dance the rugged day away

In dare-to-be-caught moments
You're not shaking like a leaf
You're swaying like a tree

DAY BREAK

We ripped free
From cities, heartbreak and work
To escape as far as we could
Before the sunset caught us
Until the sky brought down duty
Upon our chasing heads

We're desperate to tear into free
Adventures
To look, see, touch, breathe
Yet the sinking sun
Sucks us back to the city

DEMOTIVATED

The prediabetic condition
Of a breakdown

It is a creeping grip
Slowly tightening around the creative
Like some plaque-placing disease
Building through the body
Slowing the mind

Inner will shuts
Off energy
Affording no expenditure

Quiet moments grow
Passive and dull
The brain stops
Thinking simply
Only of where it's not
I could have but I can't
I would be but I'm not
Where once I came home
With all the pouncing want
To create and play
I find my will hollowed out
By work
I shrink down at
What do you do?
To an employable answer

Having sacrificed the lively hours
I couldn't sustainably extend
Beyond the boundaries of my shift

Now shrivelled by the dull grey
Spreading of my work brain
I arrive each day
demotivated

DIAMONDS IN THE DARK

Cinematic glint, ominous luxury
A sapphire opal snake eye
Twinkling with poisonous beauty
Unsustainable perfection dazzling the gaze
Sparkling like a secret in the observer who spies

The serpentine arm, veiled in darkness
Slithers silently, only drawing temptation
In green eyed glamour of watcher's greed
For the glittering oculus crowning
The jutting wrist bone

The blood thick cloak of an unlit room
Hides truth's place and shape
Chokes out the chance
For an honest look

The seer's eye leering
Runs wild, imagining
All the glitz there could be
Waiting for them in possessing looks
From the whisper of what is there

The snake eye shifts
At the dim spark in the dark
That lights the devil's gaze
Cutting sharp the blue-eyed diamond

DIGESTING MEAT

It permeates the room
The colon smell
His skin is excreting
What he will expel
He is unaware
In his comfortable norm
Of meat-eating as merely
A dietary form
Mostly I'm neutral
Supporting free choice
But his stink proves
A vomiting voice
I hold it down
Try not to judge
But my deep discomfort
Just won't budge
The undigested reek
Of decomposing flesh
Spouts further at me
On each spoken breath
I feel trapped
Sensory onslaught
Wincing at "I love you"
Despite my support
Of densely packed proteins
And heavy sweat smell
Of the food and its eater
That leaves me unwell

It's the festering stench
From his warm gut
Liquifying meat
To extrude out his butt
His freedom of choice
Is a value to me
But I wish to escape
The dead pong of meat

EXCUSE ME, I'M IN LOVE WITH YOU

Excuse me
Sorry to bother you
I know you're busy
It's not your problem
But I'm in love with you
I understand you were minding your business
And that I should do the same
But I can't stop think about you
May I ask you, well, everything?
Can I stop you every second
To ask the direction of your thoughts,
The ways of your mind?
How did you get here?
Where are you going?
Excuse me for interrupting your life
But I'd like to spend the rest of mine with you
If you tell me how to get back to my own future
I'll be on my way

FARMER'S MARKET

€5 comforts my hand
Hidden in my pocket
Secret spending power
An easy grin
Is sweetening my perusal
Giving just a friendly local feel
To immunise me
From the hard-sell
As I approach the stall

Neon card flags
Sign prices
A Westend pizzazz
That feels forced
On a cold morning

Have I become middle class,
Itching with hessian charm,
Guilty at my departure
From my working class ways?

I'm drawn to a loud farmer
With a brazen, reeling sell
I try to be brash
Let him talk me out my cash
But he tells me about his red wine
To which I am allergic
Naturally vaccinated from the purchase

I tell him my immunity
His chat instantly stops
Freed from his spiel
I move to a vegetable patch
Set out in boxes
A plastic display

I moved towards other wine-dark produce
Red kohlrabi, beetroot,
Berry-coloured cabbage
Fast fermenting my thoughts
Into jarring desires
Of pickled beets, red sauerkraut
On a kohlrabi salad
My tasty imagination
Has me whole-bodied
Oozing with ideas
My hands nearly seep out of pocket
But I spot the ginger juice
That golden compress
I'm here to buy

It bellies up the sunrise
Burning me awake each day
I beeline for its yellow glow
Shining with memories
Of morning brightness
Then I see the price tag
 "€6 per shot"

FAST TURNING FOREIGN

These fingertips
So soft, so surprising
Skate like figurines
Across my own skin
Smooth, cold, tingling
These fingertips dance
So sweetly, so seductively
As if not controlled by my mind
Slow, emotive, teasing
These fingertips had been lost
In shopping bag grips
Behind protective gloves
Forced away from my face
My family, my friends
These fingertips were fast turning foreign
Forgetting to feel
So I took a moment
For the touch of love
To feel the dramatic curve of my cheekbones
And run the edge of my budded lips
To touch my own humanness
With familiar fingertips

FLORENCE OF THE NIGHT

A bird sat on my windowsill
As I peered out of a dusking soul.
The dark seemed heavy
But here was a friend
My thoughts lifted on feathered wings

FOLDING LOBES

I feel the cold
Icky like slime
As I fold the slug
Of my earlobe in
To meet the warm
Listening cavity
That waits piously
For sound (not skin)

But when he feels the earlobe cold
A deep catharsis
Draws him inward
To a comforting place
Where children were cuddled
And snuggled to bed
After a windy family hike
Or a rainy day at home
Where he'd snuck off in the garden
Slippy and sluggy from rain
To chill his ears
Tuck them in at bedtime
And know that peace
Was only one sleep away

FOR JACK MORRIS

I've only heard your art
From afar
Your sumptuous words
Thick like tar

They pave the way
For new thought
A bloody flow
Of which I've sought

Your lines trickle
Treacle slow
In streets of mind
Everywhere they go

A footstep pattern
Heard in my head
Adding a depth
To each thought-line tread

I'd like to walk
Your world of words
Enticed to entry
By a poem I heard

FOREST ME

Entrenched in trees
I feel at ease
Slipping into the reality
Of green
I breathe
As if I were a friend
Of the forest
Like I lived here forever and then
Something moved me
Away from this natural place
That gives me the time, the space
To just be
Wholly
Immersed in me

GRADUAL GOODBYES

This is my chair and those are my trees
I shall breathe this air and watch those leaves

Then a wondrous shiver
Creeps over my head
Of regaling memories
Putting worries to bed
Where did I skydive?
Strange people, strange folk.
And those funny Australians
With whom I once spoke

Memories mix
A goodbye kiss
Blends with a moment
Of some other bliss
Bowing together, hear
Between my eyes
Every reminding photo
Is a happy surprise

Here I sit relearning
How great it is to be
Slowly falling in
To one long dream

GRANDMA'S LOCKET

In this locket
Hides a soul
It sleeps around my neck
Whispering support
Seeping comfort
Into my skin
Its metal holds the warmth
Of every heartbeat
Since the fading pulse
Within her fingers
Passed in a final tremor
Of her cooling hand

Perhaps there are built up
Beats; heart warmth
Melded into the metal
From all the years she shared
With its pendulum coeur
I wonder how she softened
The metal, beat by beat
A silversmith
This unbroken chain
And long-cherished locket
Unfastened in her hand
Her chest had an absence
When the chain slipped
Leaving dark skin
Unfamiliarly alone

I tried to reconnect
Bound around her neck
But it was broken free
Into my hands
"I want you to have it" she hushed
I took the chain, closed the loop
Around me, feeling the dying
Heat dilute into my own

GREEN EARED

I gleam with almost gratitude
As the farmer hands me the bunch
Of floppy leaves, dangling bulbous
Vegetable bodies of the field's catch
These plump little beings try
A footless escape, working as one
To spill, in canon, over the canvas
Edge of my tote
A giggle germinates in my gut
Delighting at their wriggly charisma
I gently subdue them into my bag
Adding pleasant
Weight to my shoulder-
Slung haul of goodies
Grown in the ground, delicately
Delivered from the earth
For my delectation, how royal
I feel, how humbled
At this earthbound honour
But before I reach
"Where else in the universe...?"
I first think
Of my luck in purchasing produce
Just take a handful off the shoulders
Of mass farmers drowned in demand
And pay in the earth-edged pocket
Of the small-scale farmer
Barely pricing what her wild is worth

Leave the supermarket
Shelf stocked for the penny-pinched
And pour the extra value in your stock
Of locally raised agriculture
I walk my bunny-eared bouquet home
And show it to my windowsill
Where it beams back at me
The giggle grows into a glow
A grateful warmth blossoms
Into a sweet smile, a nectar
To be shared on the streets
Homegrown grins for passersby
I marvel at how much
These plants have already given me

GREEN-VEINED GLORY

They used to be the smooshed together A's
Of my best friend's bra-bound chest
But now they have become grander
Swollen in two
Filled and fulfilling
Lying sideways on the bed
Feeding him at the fallen trunk of her
Green veined and ripe
Full of weighted meaning
And milking life for all its purpose

GRÜNER VELTINER

Photosynthetic fresh
No tannic tinge
As smooth as the cream
Of green coconuts
Holding their aroma crisp
Clean meadow with no earthen edge
This is spring clear
With only the mildest aftertaste
Of soft yuzu or citrus unsoured
There are no sharp rushes
In the air over Austrian mountains
Distilled on a clear day
Chilled into a glass
With only the faintest lime tint
To its crystalline colour
Giving a waiterly whisper
Of the rolling hills
It was pressed from

GUINNESS

It settles just before
It floods the rim
To be poured, cloud-like
Behind waiting lips

It's not here to make a scene
It's here to hold history
To make a memory
Of the impossible moment
When velvet foam
Flowing smooth
Dissipates to a woodland hush
Harking back to the home
Of every pub bench, bar and barrel
That hail its humility

Water creamed with deep wishes
Cooled like a stream
Then filled with familial warmth
No jagged minerality
Or taut tannic taste
No bovine gastric banding of the tongue
Following Bailey's

Only the hymn of hops
Fading in the mouth
Quiet, Harmonic, Mellow

HEART SHAPED POTATO

Deep in the hearth of the earth
It's grown
Enriched by the light
It's barely shown
So it twirls out its tendrils
Turgid and green
To point at the sun
That is yet unseen
Unfurling its fingers
Up to the sky
Seeking the sun
Before it's grown eyes
All of this magic
Is not light alone
There's rain and topsoil
That shape how it's grown
There's so much love
From this starchy start
That the earth-loved potato
Has the shape of a heart

HEARTY SPICE

They arrived on cinnamon air
Blending ginger in the breakfast
Blending gingers in the bed
Warming spice: a spirited life
Lighting each sunrise smile
With self-love spreading
Into deeply seasoned delight
Being adored all the while
Because they make morning porridge
Even when reminded everyday
They are loved anyway
If they stay in bed
They aren't trying to prove their worth
They aren't cooking on insecurities
There's nothing suspicious
They simply share their autumnal vim
To make life more delicious

HELPER COMPLEX: A SELF AWARE FRUSTRATION

He is sick
Dragged down by a cold
But first caught by his thoughts
Of desperation
He doesn't see the abundance
Of love surrounding him
He wants me
To make it better
He wants me
To comfort his needs
He wants me
To want him.

Is it fair to call us lovers
If he only loved me
To get me back?
I've said my sorrows
Checked what I would need for change
But he wouldn't pay it forward
And claimed his hypocrisy to be
The price of entry
So I'm leaving

But he knows I struggle
Choking on my silence
When I feel guilty of wanting to say no
Outside of helper complex eyes
Its a basic boundary
Simple respect
No regret required
But the pressure to please
That social squeeze
Holds my words hostage
Even though I am ready
For no further gratification
And to say goodbye to being needed
His forlorn face aimed at me
Humbles me down to hesitation
Despite the awareness that he is playing me
He coils up my clarity
And I feel I need to help him

HI, HE'S AN ALCOHOLIC

"I'm an alcoholic"
He says, shame circling shadows in his eyes
"Hold no blame for your past coping.
You are simply ready to change."
My warm words embrace him
But he holds the label floating before him
As if it would slip away
Leaving him to sip his way
Into the melancholic
He grips that word
With fingers clawing for accountability
2 years sober and he's barely free
Seeing its truth and truth values
But I hope one day
That it's grip sticks less
Not so that he may drink again
Or lose his groups
But so that he can chose
To identify as an alcoholic
Without the fear of his lack of will
Or need for shortcuts to social connections
But simply due to the love in his recovery

HIS MUSIC

Where there's a negative charge
My mind is a magnet - Hudson Taylor

Again, I'm one
With the full mix
Flowing through my head
As animating waves
Moving life
In fast flow
Natural, quick, crashing chaos
The splash of a cymbal
The dash to Killiney Beach
The harmony of two
Swirling and swimming
Streaming melody into one
Rolling free
As a heartbreak-happy tear
Threatens to drop
Into the beckoning depths
Of the lyrics whirling around my head
Stirring me wholly
Rushing veined rivers to sloshing heart
Aching, gushing feeling

The seas of me move again
From the cold calm
Salinated stagnation of creativity's settled dregs
For the epipelagic layer of love-made sound

HOLLYWOOD EYES

I see your eyes wandering
Chasing truth like a cloud
Grounding yourself in external
Mantras, theories, ideals
To a halt

Your self awareness has been tied up
By other tongues
Following tangled tales
Of people who want
To be heard
But have nothing to say
Their fast-fleeting logic
Swift in a trendy sky
On the winds of well-paid words

No wonder your shifty eyes won't rest
On the enlightenment within

I FEEL HIM WATCHING ME

I feel him watching me
As I moved into Warrior II
My body long, elegant
Strong
I feel like a surfer
Riding the dense excitement
Of this silent sea
His eyes glide down my neck
My narrow torso
The bareness of my legs
Eyeing the silk of my skin
I am tempted to touch its smoothness
To reach down and slide
A finger over my figure
His gaze comes like waves
Stirring me
I desire to feel
My own edges
Reaching further
Stretching deeper
Into myself
His eyes roll over my hips
And I have to steady my breath
The pull of his attention
Tickles the sloping rim
Of my pelvis
I hold my peace
Powerful and open

I breathe in stillness
Whilst an electric fire
Courses the wires of my veins
The current rushes in me
Sparks against the fluid surface
Of each spreading limb
I move into down dog
He releases me from his sight
I straighten to a stoic
Mountain
And let the ebbing embers
Fizzle at my epidermis
How wild it is
To be watched

I LOVE YOU SO MUCH

I love you so much I don't care when my phone dies.

I love you so much I would give you my stew and eat only the courgette ends.

I love you so much I really think we could outlive the sun if we just kept dancing.

I love you so much I'd work in an office of your farts just to miss you less.

I love you so much I'd miss my stop just to plant that extra kiss.

I love you so much I'd call your sexist relatives to say hello on your behalf.

I love you so much because we wiggle our bums to pretend to fly to the moon.

I love you so much because we choose to snuggle instead of eating breakfast.

I love you so much because nothing is more fulfilling than the feel of your skin.

I love you so much it gives me butterflies seven years in.

I love you.

I RESCUED A BEE

He was on the ground
Toddling an asymmetric limp
Caused by one deformed wing
I would have left him
With the ethos of an observer
Ready to watch nature at its honest best
But I couldn't help but help
Leave Noone Behind
So I found a bone dry splint
Of wood to crutch him
To his hive
After two false-start falls
I got him home
Where he could help with honey

All abilities allowed here
Help every bee

KINGFISHER

Your opulent needle
Pierces the sky
Telling me the weathered season
Is here for your hunt

The green-scented woodland chill
Ruffles ripples in the lake
Merely a material for you to cross stitch
In sharp threadlines
Anchored at your perch
Your beady eyes have taken turns
Seeking out your pinpoint prey

Now you sew: sharp, swift
Catching through the surface
Of the flowing fabric water tension
The fluid motion of a weaver
You follow back the thread
Holding the spiny stickleback in your needle
Whipstitching its end upon your spindle perch
Stripping off the spikes before swallowing
Then proudly hovering
Evening sky against sunrise morning
Wings turning to a translucent blur
As the waiting hand
Of a practised seamstress
Ready to stitch again
The pattern of life

LAKE DAY 1

Our friends are on land
It's you and I, daring to be
Hot bodies melting
The freezing lake
My legs wrapped around your waist
Locked in an undulating kiss
Desire seeping heat through
Our smouldering skin
Ferocious against the chill
Of our immersed state
You and I make it heavenly
Warmed and warming
A paradise embraced
Whispering the silhouette
Of many foreshadowed futures
Holidaying like in-love teenagers

LAKE DAY 2: WEISSENSEE

After a thousand
Tightly held breaths
Shivering through a pandemic winter
Arms clenched, surrounding
Each human bubble
Encircled and huddled, isolated
Berliners scattered like hail
Separated on the hard, grey pavement
Unmelting, unmoved

Finally flow together
Softened by the sun
Seeking no more separations
Together, as a town, tanning
Limbs spread on the Weisensee bank
Like fallen ice creams
Slowly melding together

Here lies happiness
Soft-serve, sweet, indulging
My smile beams
With sunlit teeth
Feeling friendly
As my friend and I lie nude
Modesty protected
By simple motivations
To finally feel
Sun-kissed skin

LANGUEDOC AT LA MAISON

A heavy glass
Weighted and waiting expense
First I drink in with my eyes
Imprinted clear
Roman Gaul script
Presenting the pomp
"La Maison"
Then to my nose I brush
A blushing bouquet of pink chrysanthemum
With stretched rubber scent
Reaching across my brain
Thick legs, holding the curve of the glass
Like a Bordeaux whore
Heavy peach
Then a belated punch
Ringing warm in my throat
Mark the waiter
The Dublin Restaurateur
Has made his pick
Plucked this stem
Glass for a classy customer

LEARNING TO LOVE ARGUMENTS

A thousand splits
Unnecessary separations
A million evenings lost
To sadness
Arguments used as blockades
To take sides over
Built on egos
Too cross for crossing
Over into understanding

But if we step back to the middle ground
And break down the borders
We can use the energy for from empathy
To strengthen our connection

Learn to love every argument
As the gift of growth

LIVING ROOM

2 sofas connected
By a mattress
An armchair
Plump and cuddling
Holding me in an upholstered hug
Off to the side

Included by my love
But not by rent
In my girlfriend's flat
Scattered with roommates
Who keep me included
I offer parameters, opinions
Support

Although my voice
Is bound by visitor's rights
Carrying less weight
In my gentle offered words
I'm given the time
The space to share
To contribute
I'm drawn in
To the living room

MACADAMIA NUT ICE CREAM

The great indulgence
Melting before me
Oozing its sumptuous juices
Creamy, white and sweet
Tempting me with its innocence
Untouched, unwedded
To any moistening mouth
Gelatinous cells
Hidden within trickle-sweet milk
I know the taste
And it knows I know it
Using rich, dairy gravity
To suck the memory forward
In my salivating, over-sensitive head
I'll leave the cows in peace
I'll go suck a cock
And have some cum instead

MAKING A HOME WITH YOU

Filthy, Filthy
Utterly Filthy
The whole place
Is crawling with dust motes
Teaming with tenant hairs
The our's-ness hiding unstarted
Under viscous layers of grime
We've arrived
Him, travel-tired; me, still sick
Bodies wanting to rest
But we work down to the beginning
Cleaning away cigarette ends
Feral pens
A global collection of coins
To find the raw wood
The sturdy floor
From which our home can be founded
Our thoughts don't stick
To the thick laid dirt
Because we can feel
We're moving closer
To the first day home, run
To the startline
With each cloth wipe
Vacuum sweep
Or wrist-wrecking scrub
We come further down the track
To our place of clean start

Fresh will be our haven
But warm and gentle
Padded with soft-aged furniture
And sound protecting foam
So that we can host the hottest music
Sing without burning the neighbour's walls
In happy, heartfelt song
And to avoid any emergency glass shatter
From our eardrum hammers
We the round down the corners
Of any urgency
To a gently humming heaven
Here will be the place
Where souls unfold
Not just to hold confession
But to heal the confessor
In the clear conscience orb
Of our newly loved home

MUCHA: FLOWER SKETCHES

He has, with spindle fingers, placed
The fine in arts
Pencil lines
Long, steady
Pulled up in streams
So natural, so impossible
Gathered thin, without a waver
Forming everlasting delicacy
Of a flower fresh with life
Hundreds of separate pencil strokes
Drawn so carefully, the pace and parting
Flow like brushed paint
Single gnarled lines of roots
Cobweb narrow
Unimaginably light
Crooking off from stems
Long ribbed shading
Tender and true
Holding the fragility
Of life

MUSHROOM SOUP AT FRAUENHUEBER

Grey-flecked and oil-specked
Leaving a crumbled gravestone trail
Down the side of my bowl
At first presenting white foam
Some J.W.Turner sky
Hiding its pebble
Of well-blended soup
The flavour is so creamy
Its minerality ground smooth
With a buttery finish
Melting my mouth's cave
Every morsel of mushroom
Folds modestly into my tongue
Ending its impact on the world
With a murmur of flavour
Before fading with a bow
Into my grateful greater body

MUSIC AT THE RESTAURANT
OBENCNI DŮM

The arch and bow of art deco
Echoes all around
Dancing to the bouncing swing
Of wood-muted brass
Big band records of the past
An oboe solos and sighs
When the bobbing tuba
Or percussive piano arise
To take back vintage velvet thick sway
Playing upon diners' [ear]drums
Gently, soft as a misbegotten memory
Even the duck beak daffy trumpets
Dampen to a low gold
Wrapping a gilded glimmer
Around the glass pencils
Of 3 tiered tassel skirted chandeliers
7 white pill-shaped lights
Suspended in a golden ring
Wedded forever to the past years
In the house of ever-dying swing
As pills come alive
Their bulbs raise aged warmth
People flow in to fill reservations
The hall begins to twinkle
Giving patrons a champagne stain
Melding them with the woodwork

I feel a hand-me-down nostalgia
As I am hearing back in time

MY BALCONY GARDEN

She sat plucking a dying babe
From the plants her balcony made

Parsley's having a really hard time
So she cut out the trying, to help, leaves

Snip snip, start again
My growing sister, my glowing friend

MY SCAR IS STRETCHING

My scar is stretching
Spreading beyond the neat bounds
Of methodical med-school stitches
Into a shiny blur of ripple-tight tissue

It is spreading because I ignored it
It is spreading because I didn't rest
It is spreading because I lost the steristrips
And let it loose in my life

Exposed and unsupported
Forced to heal in flux
Leaving a growing smudge
Of permanent damage

I'm scared to stop moving
Scared I'll lose momentum
Believing 'rest' and 'productivity'
Are mutually exclusive

Only now can I see the tears
Here, they are skin deep
But I feel wounds howling
In the curtailed core of me
Because with every imperfection
I learned only to cut it out

MY WORDS ARE LIKE RABBITS

My words like rabbits
Returning to the burrows
Of his soft-fold ears
Leaving them a little more fur-lined
At each homebound tale
Over the years, his ears fluff with stories
Making it harder to hear
Their muted feet in storied step

NAPPING TOGETHER

A dimension has been lifted
We're so light, we're hovering
On the edge of embodiment
Teetering before the tumble
Out of time-trapped reality
Everything is so

       o

         o

          o

           o

             soft

I'm barely aware
Of my concave waist
Capping his thigh
And his unconscious thoughts
Connecting us, creating
A symbiosis of warmth

Blissful drifter
This last thought is for you

NOSTALGIA LIKE HONEY

Nostalgia at the beehive
Sussurating like an old TV
Reminding me of the 90s
When I would roam
Barefoot child
Returning home
Only once the sun threatened
To lay down for the night
Where my grass-stained knees
And mud-speckled ankles
Were so much closer
When I laid outstretched in meadows
Bees were my friends
And remain so now

Commuting around me
With a universal business
That endless black, yellow
White noise
Hums me to a trance
Some eternal tranquillity
That brings a tear to my eyes
I could stay still forever
Held long and loose
In sound
Calmed by their chaos
And feeling statuesque by comparison
But the smell is so inviting

The ancient dry, flaky wood
Saturated in sticky nectar
The sumptuous oozings
Of a thousand flowers
Is too tempting
I'm buzzed in by the scent
Allowed to trespass unpunish
To hang my nose before the hive
Hovering, eyes shut
On the warm candle smell

I'm not afraid of being stung
Even as a human stinking being
The buzzing traffic lemons
Around my slow-incoming head
I am too bliss out to be a threat
They know they have enchanted me
I'm a happy child again
Welcomed to the hive

ODE TO THE INTROVERT

Simply given time
To be still
My thoughts and ideas
Are the greatest thrill
Through infinite wandering
There's no time to kill
Alone I am occupied
No social needs to fill

OLD IRISH FORESTS

Hawthorn, Holly
Birch, oak and rowan
For the love of the land
Keep the forests going
Take out your spades
Let the earth hug the seeds
For rolling green landscapes
Of thousands of trees

Once there were timbers
Over soft topsoil
So alive, so turgid
Never seeming to spoil
The biosphere had
A threat of disease
That was spread thin
Over many species

Homogenous planting
Replaced diversity
Affecting the soil
As well as the trees
Foreign rulers
Replaced the yule
To export new wood
For building and fuel
Where creatures could ceilidh
From coast to coast

Of all that was taken
The forest lost the most
Of the native forests
That were once present
Ireland is left
With 1.5 percent

OUR FIRST SHOW

I stand beside you
In a room full of love
My heart shakely opening
Into the twinkle-lit space
Welcomed by familiar smiles
Of friends sticking thicker than blood
Looking up at our hopes
The dreams they believed in
And called forth
I can hear my fears creeping in
But I hold my key
I sing myself centred
Let the flow take me
My new career begins
Right on the stage
Ignited by the audience's faith
In our music, your guitar
My words, our voice
This is the start

PALM HEARTS

A tenderness vowed to the ancients
A platonic form to white asparagus
Playing in the heaven space
Between divine threads of vegetal robes
And a heart textured so soft
It's already tongue mushed and gone
Yet that middle draws out all the mmm's
Delight, slides loose from Seraphic core
Angel hairs rest in the impossibly smooth
Shaft of a sweetly moulded cylinder
Shaped through palm forest's
Photosynthetic pulse

If the sweetness of love is held in the heart
This is the fruit of loveliness

PESTO

Garlic pureed to cream
Mixed to a cloud of basil
Soft crumble soaked parmesan
Cashews instead of pine nuts
Kissed by the zesty love of lemon
So delicate I take extra home
In a scalloped shell
Ready to paint my mouth once more
In serene Botticelli seas
Of tender greens
With this fresh moment
My mouth falls in love
At La Maison

PICKLED SKIN

My cheeks are pebbled
With tiny constellations
Cystic clusters
Guiding my body
Through the journey to immunity
Gift from the state
Through an invasive dose
Of liberty
Straight into the muscle
Of alms
Now painful, swollen
Red reactionary grace
My vaccine sunk below the surface
Spreading through me
To protect my body from the disease
That has ravished our last 18 months
Looking after me only
As a pin holding
Up the economy

PINS AND NEEDLES

My leg, my foot
Have gone to sleep
Trading tender touch
For tingles
In a heavy creep

I try to stand
But they're weighted firm
And my slow-wiggle toes
Must come to terms

With my waking knock
And heavy limb shake
Forcing my blood
To recirculate

But before jarred joints
Start to cease
My hot stomp banging
Is just the squeeze

To pump my blood
From toe to knee
Then back around
My whole body

78 PLEASE GO ABROAD BEFORE MY HEART BREAKS

I'll just love you
That's all I can do
I can't fix you, I can't break you
I can't stop you, I can't make you
When wings are your mode, feelings are feathers,
Whatever I feel, we won't be together
Rise up once more, flying above
Follow your dreams
And leave me with love

PONDERING PONDEROSA

A weedward salad
With a wayward soup
Take an extra twenty
Type of delicious
And all we need to do
Is digest
Enjoying the green
By the eye
The gut
The nose
The lungs
The heart
The mind
Take it slow
Unwind

People are here; not prices
The grounds are fertile
With their singing, laughing
Dancing, toiling hands
The languid earth
Grows a bounty
At every footred
Thanks to the greeting grasp
Of gallant hippies
Bathing, coddling and haircutting
The wild abundance
That surrounds homemade housing

All is slow progress
Gently changing
At the rate of seasons
Nothing is agitated
Not even the rice milk
Will submit to urging
At the coffee machine foamer
Take everything soft and smooth
At Ponderosa

POP BY AT WORK

Shake me from routine
With your Saturday morning smile
On a soggy Friday afternoon
Haul me out
From my hunched working mind
Grey and blocky, like these buildings
Give me a tangible kiss
Wrap your arm around mine
And lead me to a cuddle spot
Tell me it makes your day to see me
If only for a break

POST-VACCINE FLU

Gratitude
Focus on gratitude
My body is in turmoil
Learning this new sickness
From the cadavers of old cells
Spiky nausea is sitting
Below the surface of my skin
Liquidating my flesh
Into trembling, aching putty
The bone of my skull
Gushing with tightness
Echoes rushing sounds
Pressed upon my ears
But I'm grateful for this fever
Thankful for this freedom
Set out in immunity
And the studying of my body
From old cells to protect the new

RAPESEED FIELDS AND INFANT WHEAT

The world gushes by
In oceans of yellow
Rapeseed fields
Green seas of infant wheat
I want to wade, to front crawl across
The tickle-brush tendrils
Of bright, swaying growth
Moved by tide-like winds
But rooted in the bedrock earth
I want to feel the cool
Touch rush
Over my skin
As I dive in
And swim out
To somewhere far
Beyond the horizon

RED VEINS

Held up by baluster fingers
Leaved and licked
By the wam lap
Of dog-happy sun
Flat they lay
Each languid leaf
Glowing red in afternoon
Shining autumn
With photosynthetic sparkles
Embracing a corner
Of a crumbly home
The turgid strength of vines
Scaffolding the walls melting
Into their tender hug
The hearts grown in this house
Have flourished safe
Under growing support
Of red veins, respiring still
Pumping life back into bricks
That would otherwise fall
As the rubble of a silenced home
Where no longer
Hearts are grown

RESEARCH

A rising irritation
Wrangles my muscles
Threatening to pull me
Forcibly from the chair
I'm desperate to dance,
To move, to spring and escape
From self-captivity
But I'm stuck on a numbing butt

I'm studying, researching,
For a self-inflicted project
The inviting sun seduces my periphery
And my body involuntarily turns
Towards the enticing rays

But my arse remains magnetised
To my undeterred seat,
With the wood-solid soul,
Of my researcher's will
To endlessly know
The hard-to-find facts
Stuck in the corners of time
Barely reachable
Even with the vacuum
Of my hours
Pedantically searching
For answers I don't need
Yet burn for no less

The sun warms my cheek
With a motherly touch
Reminding me I'm embodied
And need to eat, sleep
Breathe

I finish scribbling a note
On some faint echo quote
Of some forgotten person
And move as if I will stand

Then I read a little more
And sink back down
To dissect just one page more

RUNNING DOWN STAIRS

Crush, trample, kick, thunder
Bearing the weight of motion's wonder
Stamp, tread, totter, slip
Cycling the stairs, pedal each hip
Run, sprint, jump, jog
Racing my heart through the fog
Carry, catch, cushion, cruise
My balance suddenly floats loose
Swing, sway, step, stumble
The torrid of feet fall and fumble
Plummet, plunge, stop, sit
Crack in my phone screen
"Oh shit"

SALMON TARTARE AT CERNA MODERNA

Salmon with its soft edges
Even softer flavour
Is cubed against the sweet embrace
Seaweed salad strips
Peppered with speck-sized nasturtium
Topped with a bean sprout crunch
Like a spring water crisp in the ocean
A drop of the gentlest mustard jus
Flowing through aquatic tastes
In my mouth-bound terrarium
Light, bright and raw edge soft
The clear, sweet mallow
Of membranes grown at sea
Below the waves
Lies the succulent meadows
Blissful, calm and mellow

SAUV' BLANC LES FUMÉES BLANCHES LURTON

Where's foretelling taste
Of revenge?
Where is the foreboding
Before my liver starts eroding,
When tomorrow
Claws back control
From my freewheeling hands,
Leaving a just burn
Down my gullet
And a hole in my wallet?

At the restaurant Obencni Dům
The glass of white
Looks uncolored by expense
To my prying and pricing eye.

This chaotic neutral wine
Drinks like spring-innocent water.
It is idyllic liquid
Untainted by tannins
Or on-coming consequence
Until the last legs
Down the glass
Join the dram
At its juicy crux
To reveal pure poison

SKIN ON SPUDS

Keep the story of where it's from
Keep the flavour from where it's come
Keep the potato skin on

Carve it up and fry it quick
Cut the spud finger thick
Or julienned to a matchstick
Keep the skin on

Hit the frier or the pan
Keep it crisp as best you can
Soggy fries deserve a ban
Keep the skin on

Give me fries with taste left in
Peeling is a pious sin
Lightly salted and searing
Keep the skin on

STABBING NAILS

A red scab dances on my face
First on my chin
Then on my cheek
Bouncing back and forth
Between forehead and nose
I try to ignore it
But it punctuates my zoom calls
A glitch in my attention
I stare at its pixels
Willing it away
I'm the one who put it there
With perfectionist fingers
That scratch, pick and squeeze
The most invisible blackhead
Becomes a ripped open scrape
As my stabbing nails
Corner my flesh
Forcing it to surrender
Staked-out, snaked-out sebum
My skin is mostly beautiful
Clear and supple
Hepburn Haut
Yet my nails work against me
Against my sweet expelling surface
They amplify an unnoticeable blemish
Into an eye-drawing blotch
When will I learn
To leave my epidermis alone?

SUNSET SALAD

I'm sure I can taste the orange
Setting sun in my food
Turning dressed edges
Of my salad to sweet
Amber touched mustard
Honey and oil
Sap-like coating on crispy leaves
Plucked mere metres
From this crumble-crafted bench

Lettuce life crackles
Between my teeth
As I crunch up the leaves
Of this sunraised meal

I can taste the whole spectrum
Of light-lifted mouthfuls
Feel the refreshing flavours
Mingle with low flame sun glows
Dripping over the lip
Of my glistening evening mouth

THE BROCCOLI IN OUR LIVING ROOM

I make a pasta
Orange rind, ginger skin
Randomly delicious
But thrown together with care
Quality checked by qualified taste buds
Who learned to learn
From tongue scraping mistakes

This homemade meal is part living room
Having wilted down leafy scraps
Of our wieldy weedward broccoli
That has tangled its tendrils
Over the corner of out couch
It's fibrous stems curve
Coiling tubers around cornicing
Sprouting its flora behind the curtains
In window winding with vim
Spreading out an abundance of leaves
That eventually reach the dinner table
In boiled surrender

The 5 foot plant pays its leaves of green
As rent, contributing to the cooking

THE CHILDREN WON'T COMMUTE

It's raining, it's pouring
The whole world is snoring,
Asleep to the thunderous rain.
As it pours outside,
Its ever-faithful bride
Is the earth
And they meet once again.

In festive spirit, the plants shall grow,
Dancing towards the sky.
Reaching up to the rain
In a variety show
Of green-veined hands held high.

But among this fest
The shadow-shufflers form
Sucking air from the breeze block grey.
Their lethargic commute
In the cross-hatching storm
Is the snoring start to their day.

The time from their mornings
Seems to drip down the drain
As their hair starts to undress.
When the sun returns
Their work-weighted mind
Seems dampened no less.
To brighten the grey

Children can advise
Because the children know
To look with fresh eyes.
They spin with their fingers
Held up to the clouds;
Bridesmaids
To the green-fingered ground.
Their dancing feet
Make a joyous sound:
A gentle pitter-patter
All around

THE FIRST MORNING TOGETHER AGAIN

2 chests sliding
Side by side
1 arm wrapping
A shallow-thin shoulder
The torso, the belly
Holding happy morning peace
Calmly, relaxed in love
Dappled sound of birdsong
Passing over the naked lovers
As they rest on a rising sun
The world seems gentle
4 closed eyes, 2 open hearts
They breathe in and out
With togetherness
Neither wanting for anymore
Or any less
Both feeling beautiful
Mind, soul and skin
In sync
Coupled in an eternal moment

THE LOST ART OF HEMBRAIDING

This skirt has combed the earth
So long
Its edges fraying
Breaking off as teeth
Now the ground grinds them down
Shrinking back its once elegant gape
Chewing slowly with each brush
Until the grimacing row
Must be cut away
Raw edge felled
Tucking back gum-hole gaps

But this time a loving hand
Wraps the fold in an embrace
Of thick taffeta
Touching care, protecting
A tender lip
To boldly roam, confidently comb
The earth again

THE LOVE OF A FRIEND

I'm wrapped inside his coat
Waiting together for my train
Cheek pressed to the hidden heart
Behind a cuddly jumper
Echoing his cuddly soul

Here is a human so full of love
He bursts through social norms' seams
Explodes away from the haute commitment
To wholly commit only to the moment
Sharing deep love within it
Damning norms as a cage
Built on arcane insecurities
And relationship hierarchy
Yet he loves all the deeper with freedom

He loves like no one loves
He shares like no one shares
Giving all he has as far as he can
Stretching the love of his past partners
Into tender years of growing,
Passionate friendships
Treating their new partners
As a gift he is ever grateful for
So when the mind is urging to ask
"Where do I fit in his ocean of love?"
It hasn't let go of love as a backyard pond
Quaint and hidden from the world

Only for one household

The unimaginable depths of his
Romantic care multiply
Into engulfing waves of kindness
Passion, compassion and compersion

So when you stop thinking you'll drown
Without being pulled up
To some mountainous hierarchy beside him
By a solid label and a crumble-free status
You'll find you have all you need and more
More movement, more freedom
As one of his many fish
Beloved and each wholly held
If you stop underestimating
The pacific size of his love

THE OLD ACHE OF INSECURITY

I want to tuck inside his life
Like a treasured pocketbook
Only lying open
At his secreting hands
A finger resting teasingly
On my central crease
To usher forth precious stories
Of a life lived by the heart
Hold me for a lifetime
Bound by gentle care
Closed to other readers eyes
Let me be yours to smile over
Let my pages only yellow
When you have loved them each
In a thousand intimate moments
Let me suffer only
The beating
Of your heart

THE PLIGHT OF 1 PLY

Everywhere in Prague
When I went to the loo
I found the TP rather thin
Each time I did a poo

The city is upheld
By 1 ply totem poles
But chiffon thin paper
Makes me use an entire roll

Perhaps I could support it
Even though I found it strange
If it were some kind of effort
To tackle climate change

We'd use less plastic shipping
Fewer bathroom scrolls
So Prague perhaps up the ply
On all your toilet rolls

THE RUST ON GRANDPA'S TIN TOOLS

Left in the shed, I crumbled
Old red epidermis decayed
Pocked skin exposed
Heart echoing the last beat of love.
Was my solidity assumed?
I defy your inanimate ideas
Of me sitting as you left me
I flake as I wait.

Could I fall away to nothing
And escape being
In neglect?
My carapace is cold
Without him to hold me.

I'm not just a tool.
This tin has a heart.

THE SCENTED STREETS OF VIENNA

I whirled around
At the thick oak scent
Releasing a trailing sentence
Through the flick of my hair
"I smell cigar smoke"

My words blow back at me
As the amber brown limb
And tan moccasin
Of the smoker juts
From his Discovery Sport

An opulent branch
Shouldering antiquity
Thickened the air
With mahogany sumption

This is not the gentle papyrus
Of ancient libraries
Of the thick forest choke
Of burning wood
The aroma presents the sense
Of a gentleman's office
Where caramel sweet sunlight
Glowing on the smooth wooden base
Of a curve legged chair

And puff of upholstery
Add a bristling oud
To the decadent musk
Drawing one into its olfactory opera

A horse drawn carriage trundles tourists
Musically around a corner
I suck in the click-clack whiff
As it mingles with the chocolatey smoke
Wishing for the spiky ammonia edge
Of some drunkard's urine
To fill the last corner piece
As I smell back in time

THE TIME TO READ

No luxury sinks under my skin
Or soaks me wholly with pious delight
Or lifts me into floating gaiety
Like the time to read

Nothing else raises me up
To heights of pleasure
Dizzying to consider
Venturing down from
Let alone stepping away
From its immersive grace

Let me remain a tableau
My most timeless unaging state
Where all that expands are numbers
On each page

Let me be the sitter
For stories to be printed upon
Let me be the muse
For time to stand still and paint
In other histories

When I rejoin other people's 'now'
I'll listen to them with the intensity
Of learning a new book

THICK FOAM MORNING

(Read slowly with a cappuccino)

It pads my lip like a pillow

Cushioning the morning

In soft beige

From the stark rays

Of wake up sunshine

Taking sweet filler dreams

Turning them softly

Into caffeine

Slipping wakefulness

Under a milky cloud

So as not to shift me from sleep

With the hot shock

Of an Americano

TICKLE

2 adults
A serious couch
With well-matched cushions
And plain clothes
Erupting giddy
In breath-catching laughter

With scurrying fingers
Speeding over each other's skin
Squealing and squirming
Wriggling escape
The 2 tussle
In wheeze-worthy joy
Tickling with teasing hands
Twinkling eyes

2 adults
A jump-up-and-down-able couch
With throwable cushions
And riding up clothes
Bursting as children
In breath-catching laughter

TO DRAW FROM EXPERIENCE

I see your miseries like black ink
Waiting to scribe beautiful poetry
Decadent staves of music
From sparrows song to goosebump chorale
Or capturing stories that hold the reader
In Stockholm syndrome

Your opaque pain can paint the curves
Of Gothic buildings or beautiful pictures
It can fill the world with a painterly edge
Of all that you see, understand and hope for
It can outline the changes you wish to make
And draw forth the future you wish to fetch

From each left-to-right line
Of your past-shadow ink
I would like to help you process pain
To break it down to smooth
Fluid from its futility
From the charcoal block you achingly hold
In your shadow-ebbing body

Together we can crumble it
Every precious art supply
And turn the world achingly beautiful
As it upholds the sparkling highlights
Of a life shared
With the empowerment of love

TOENAILS

I never liked toenails
Their dirt catching curve
Their hateful snaggle blade
Their self fladulating wings

They bite the hand
That chops them back

So I have clipped and clamped
Cutting and tearing
On straight and daring diagonals
Just to bring them in line

But my loathing urges my hand too far
I find my boundaries running wild
Starting a war against the nail
Forcing a white-nail-edge flag
To fly in surrender

But even in bloodshed
Of the flesh caught in the wrath
The war seems unsettled
I know the nail will dare to take back
The territory of my toe

TOMATEN ESSENZ AT THE WALDORF

3 ravioli, black tapenade
Bobbing, barely above room temperature
In tomato bath water

The black olive bitter
In mildly astringent mead
Reminds the tongue of tartness
Forgets the turgid freshness
Skin cracking essence
Of fresh tomato

Floating somewhere distant
In the shallow-filled bowl
A textbook chef
Surface deep
Has undercooked the pasta
Overestimating how the teig
Would melt in passionless tepidity

Neither consumer nor ingredients are moved
By the aftermath of some sad tomato's ablutions
Only at the cold dregs of this silver-spooned drink
Does the memory of a tomato come to mind
But this is by no means tomato "Essenz"
This is the spiritless aftermath of a heartless soup

ROAD TRIP TO POLAND

We only meant to go for an hour
To Chorin from Berlin
But now we're in Küstrin
Having passed passport free
In a pandemie
Amongst the witch-finger trees
In traveller's glee, just us three

Radio singing
Melodic mumbling
around well-known choruses
But we're pushing beyond the boundaries
Demanding an adventure
Accept us not just in your nature
But also to pass through your war-
Torn walls
As the ghosts of freedom
The world has been whispering about

We drive by a football match slowly
Lapping up stares
Poured over our licence plate
The car feels like it's flying
On broken rules
I only want to go back
When we have circled the whole earth

TRUSTING HIM

He's at the wheel
Perfect slender fingers
Winding us out of the city
Slapping the plastic steer
In time to the radio

I watch with vignetted focus
Each smooth nail,
Each crinkle covered knuckle
And tiny, fine hairs
Animating each digit's dance

Calm energy rises in me
Turned on and blissful
Imagining where those hands could take me
What they could do there

I don't know where we're going
But I'm in his hands now

WAKAME SALAD

Green goma wakame
Slivers of delicious joy
Sweet and tangy
A juicy crunch
Unrelenting pleasure
In my begging mouth

Each day-glo thread
Ties my senses
In momentary bliss
Absorbing my attention
In mermaid-hair finery

Slowly, I chomp
Through ethereal delight
Indulging every second
With awareness

As soon as I swallow
Gratitude floods me
For foreign flavours
Being so familiar

WEDNESDAY MORNING

I am lavished
In sweet generosity
The noble freedom
Of sharing humble tea
With a dearest friend
A person I choose
Rather than a business body
To which I'm held loose
I am here seen
Gleefully heard
For a friend finds the youness
That falls between words

That I can sit with the monstera
Watching cold morning sun
In the puzzle piece apartment
Of a dearly loved one
Is a whole-hearted joy
And much needed relief
From the ongoing undeserving
I'd held as belief
I was taught as a child
That you are what you earn
By now as an adult
It's time to unlearn
And take back my mornings
My cold afternoons
For sharing friendship

Or letting love bloom

Today is Wednesday
And I'm allowed to just be
Not to force out my tiredness
With endless coffee

I can sit with autonomy
Or hit the yoga mat
Or go for a walk
Or call for a chat
But whatever I do
It's not for someone else
Or something I rush through
Doing in stealth

Today is my Wednesday
Though this freedom may pass
I will enjoy every moment
For as long as it lasts

WHEN MY LOVER WATCHED ME FALL IN LOVE WITH ANOTHER WORLD

I hear ballet notes in high beamed air
Like Degas dancers in Edvard Munch colours
At each semitone tendu
A portamento carried my soul
Over the muted press of each key
Over the airish saint's hands
Over the piano pew
And whirling fingers
Drawing twirls in the air

The space is full of hymnic heaven
The gates are upright strings
I felt my spirit lift as it entered
The world of sound; the only world I feel real
An unknown sense of belonging
Enlightens me as I pass
Into music

Wordlessly, the lover with me watches
My spirit go
Trailing only tears on my corpse's cheek.
He leaves me

WINE

My sancerre slips
Like a snake
Down my esophageal slalom
Gelling in my gut
As a viscous post-orgasmic juice
Its sweet remnants ruminating
On my raft of a tongue
Boating on an ocean
Of wine-tipped words
Floating across the restaurant
On breath-filled sails
Its dry sweet perfume
Permeates stiff marble
Softening our table
To a gem-crushed velvet
Smooth and tender to finger's touch
Serpentine transformations
In the crystalline curves
Upholding that holy cup
From which this sinning eve can sip
Soaking in sin at each swallow
Of fruitful delight
To merge and flow
Under divine influence
Susurrating with pleasure

YOUR JUMPER; A TOKEN OF YOU

I like to wander with you
By my side, swinging between the seams
Of your fabric periphery
Holding my arms
Cuddling my core
Enwrapped in you
Your obnoxious colours
Their too-bold print
The looseness you insist on
Hanging huge on me
Hanging out with me, as a jumper

I wear you wishing for your hand
I wear you watching your videos
I wear you playing with my memories
I'll wash you and wish I hadn't
Because the cotton warmth
That holds me in your scent
Will fade

YOUR KEY

I find my fingers fiddling
Coiling and uncoiling
Around the comfort of your key
The one you gave me
Knelt by the duvet
Whilst I was blinking through my bedhead
My 80's lion's mane
Half delivered from sleep
But you woke me with a dream
Of a thing to hold when I'm losing my grip
Through the tiredness of my day
When the hourly timer runs out
And I find my mind wobbling to an
I can't do this anymore
The resilient metal chimes at me
Clinking against my work keys
And reminding me of my strength
Of your love
When my well-worked knees
Begin to buckle
Under the piling hours
My finger rims the keyring
Daring to slip into its sturdy circle
And bring me back
To a bedbound moment
Unlocking my imagination
Uncaging me from my job
To think of when your arms

Will encircle me again

The key you gave me shines
Against the dull grey of my work
Offering a newness
Within the familiar feel
Of what I always carry with me
There's a token of you to cherish
A token of trust and partnership
That reminds me of my moreness
When I feel I'm just a worker

Here is the key that lets me in
To your love and home
Here is the key that lets me know
I am loved and not alone